11070 0876

ROTC Kills

Also by John Koethe

POETRY

Blue Vents

Domes

The Late Wisconsin Spring

Falling Water

The Constructor

North Point North: New and Selected Poems

Sally's Hair

Ninety-fifth Street

PHILOSOPHY

The Continuity of Wittgenstein's Thought

Scepticism, Knowledge, and Forms of Reasoning

ESSAYS

Poetry at One Remove

ROTC Kills

⇥ poems ⇤

John Koethe

HARPER ● PERENNIAL

NEW YORK ● LONDON ● TORONTO ● SYDNEY ● NEW DELHI ● AUCKLAND

HARPER  PERENNIAL

ROTC KILLS. Copyright © 2012 by John Koethe. All rights reserved. Printed in
the United States of America. No part of this book may be used or reproduced
in any manner whatsoever without written permission except in the case of
brief quotations embodied in critical articles and reviews. For information ad-
dress HarperCollins Publishers, 10 East 53rd Street, New York, NY 10022.

HarperCollins books may be purchased for educational, business, or sales
promotional use. For information please write: Special Markets Department,
HarperCollins Publishers, 10 East 53rd Street, New York, NY 10022.

FIRST EDITION

Designed by William Ruoto

Library of Congress Cataloging-in-Publication Data is available upon request.

ISBN 978-0-06-213602-2

12 13 14 15 16 OV/RRD 10 9 8 7 6 5 4 3 2 1

To John and Annie

CONTENTS

ACKNOWLEDGMENTS

Some of the poems in this book have appeared in the following journals or magazines:

The American Scholar: "Analogies and Metaphors," "*The Great Gatsby*," "The Red Shoes"

Boston Review: "ROTC Kills"

Columbia: "Arthur," "1135," "The Specious Present"

The Cortland Review: "In the Emergency Room"

Court Green: "Alfred Hitchcock"

The Harvard Advocate: "The Poem of the Mind"

Jacket2: "The Whole Creation"

The Kenyon Review: "Watchful Waiting"

The New Republic: "Stele"

Poetry: "Book X," "Like Gods"

Southwest Review: "Burnished Days," "Locus Solus"

The Virginia Quarterly Review: "Eggheads," "Self-Portrait on YouTube"

The Yale Review: "The Emergence of the Human"

"The End of the Line" was published as a broadside by the 2010 Beall Poetry Festival at Baylor University.

"*The Great Gatsby*" was commissioned by the Port Authority of New York and New Jersey and first published in *A Poetic Celebration of the Hudson River* to commemorate the quadricentennial in 2009 of Henry Hudson's discovery of the river that now bears his name.

"The Whole Creation" was first published in *Harold Bloom*80*, a chapbook celebrating Harold Bloom's eightieth birthday published in 2010 by Yale University.

"Alfred Hitchcock" was reprinted on the website Poetry Daily.

The last paragraph of "Book X" is taken from the conclusion of Plato's *Phaedo*, in G. M. A. Grube's translation as revised by John Cooper.

The epigraphs of four of these poems are taken from earlier poems of my own: that of "The Bean House" is from "A Parking Lot with Trees"; that of "Burnished Days" is from "The Substitute for Time"; that of "Dreams at Sixty-Five" is from "In the Park"; and that of "Watchful Waiting" is from "North Point North."

I would like to thank Dana Prescott and the staff of Civitella Ranieri, where some of the poems in this book were written.

ROTC Kills

THE END OF THE LINE

There are feelings you expect to have
And satisfactions you hope to find
In the course of an ordinary day, as it unwinds
From the faint morning light and morning
Paper through a mild spring afternoon, and evening,
Dinner, music, then the drink before bedtime,
When you turn off the lights. And then there are
Those moments that destabilize the day, like that near
Miss in the car—a premonition of eternity in time,
The sudden stab of fear that I may cease to be.
I make my way across the page on which I find myself
Confined, a cipher at the center of the story,
Tracing out the outlines of these never-ending
Sentences that define my life, and always haunted
By the inkling of that world beyond the mind,
Beyond the poem of the mind, the poem of *my* mind,
Where I don't exist, and life goes on without me;
The impossible world from which I'm absent,
Waiting there in the blank space at the end of the line.

ANALOGIES AND METAPHORS

I want to get out of myself and what I've written,
Yet I wear each moment like a hat. The brim,
The feather stuck in the hatband—what do *they* mean?
What kind of metaphor is *that*? What kind of hat?
I remember an essay I wrote in Luther League
About the soul's journey towards salvation: like a rocket,
I said (it was just after Sputnik), a three-stage rocket
Fueled by discipline and faith (the hydrogen and oxygen)
That roars inexorably aloft until the third stage fires
And the satellite separates and the soul settles into its orbit
Around God, emitting little beeps of praise. "Analogies,"
Said Pastor Paul, "are fine, but never take one to its logical
    conclusion."

Who needs an MFA when you have Pastor Paul?
I was raised Catholic, then my mother restaged the
    Reformation
And we all became Lutherans, but I'm indifferent to that now.
What passes for religion in my life is whatever these syllables
    portend

As your eye moves down the page, following a train of memory
and thought
To its nonconclusion in a momentary state of mind. All
around me
Life pursues the uneventful course that physics sets,
While I navigate another Easter Sunday time and entropy
Are already starting to dissolve—like someone become so
immune
To disappointment that it doesn't hurt, for whom salvation lies
In a resistance to reality, in analogies and metaphors that give
life shape,
Because the truth is inert. I sometimes used to feel
There was something missing, but I think I'm over that.
The day is wide and meaningless. I doff my hat.

THE REALITY OF THE PAST

My first sense that there was something fishy about memory and time came when I was running track in high school. I was better at speed than distance, and towards the end of a 220 or 440 the pain in my thighs would become unbearable (a lactic acid buildup), yet though I could remember nearly every detail of the race—the look and feel of the track as I settled into the blocks, the sound of the starter's gun, the way the other runners appeared to me as I blew by them or they passed me, the bright white tape—when I thought back on it I could never call to mind the actual feeling of that pain, of that excruciating pain. It was as though it had vanished not just from my memory of the past, but from the past itself. How can something so intense be so elusive? And the question generalizes: How much of what we call "experience" is just an aspect of the present, no more real than that, and beyond the concepts we possess to capture or retain? It generalizes further: Is the individual life each of us prizes as his own a fact at all? It celebrates itself, but then eventually it ends, its perspective disappears, it fades from others' memories and then from time itself, from that dehumanizing structure where it dreamed itself alive, bare ruin'd choir where late the sweet birds sang. I'm back in high school. None of this has crossed my mind, the future stretches out before me, substantial and determinate as the life I'm going to have. I stretch, I do some wind sprints. The sun is brilliant and the sky is blue. I'm hanging out with Tom and Ed and Richard in the shade beneath the bleachers, waiting for the relay to start. I'm seventeen. The race is about to begin.

"The Reality of the Past" is a paper by the philosopher Michael Dummett that I first read thirty years ago. I'd been in the doldrums, casting about for ideas to engage me (I'm better at reacting to ideas than at having them). The paper's central argument is elaborate and compelling, its conclusion unconvincing (it's philosophy after all): that the past is not, in some sense, wholly "there," in much the way that Aristotle thought the future isn't there at all. Bear with me. Yes, of course we talk and think about the past, and some of what we say and think is true; the real question is what makes it true. A text of moments stretching backwards endlessly and fixed for all eternity, that bears no trace of us and lies beyond our limited capacity to read? Or something that can breathe and speak to us, that leaves behind the possibility that it might speak to us again? Perhaps it all comes down to temperament, to where you feel at home: an austere vision of the world in which this little life is nothing and experience a dream; or a dream in which it's everything, and life is all. The mind is always present, nothing lasts, all else remains in doubt. And as for what tomorrow might contain, there isn't much to say and less to choose: tomorrow is unrealized, and since the past is nothing but tomorrow seen through time's reversing lens, the choice is not a real one at all, between the future's hazy possibilities and the ghostly consolations of the past.

"That was a way of putting it—not very satisfactory." Wittgenstein, in those "mystical" remarks at the end of *Tractatus*, says that if eternity is timelessness, as opposed to infinite duration, then eternal life belongs to those who live completely in the present. What might that mean? To be free from both anxiety and regret, from anticipation of what's still to come and disappointment at the way one's life went up to now? What matters isn't what time is, but how it feels in passing—which is a way of saying "time" means two entirely different things: the time of the cosmologists and the time in which a person's life unfolds. I live inside the latter, which begins and ends with me. And since its past is made of memories, to live completely in the present is to live without remembering, so that eternal life would be a kind of half life, not a real life at all. What is a real life? One summed up in a story, however commonplace and uninspired, that holds together all its passing parts? I'm sitting at my desk, looking out the window from the vantage point of sixty-four. It's September, there's a hint of color in the leaves, and at the same time I'm still sitting in the cool shade beneath the bleachers on an April afternoon in nineteen sixty-three, still waiting for the relay to begin. The course lies straight before me, for although I couldn't see it then, I see it now. The stages of a life make up, in retrospect, a world as real as any world could be, but self-contained. I know it's finally going to disappear "into libraries, onto microfilm," and then into a common atmosphere that anyone can breathe. It's such an intimate eternity, in which time's arrow is determined not by entropy but by memory, where anything that happened once can happen once again, and where to be alive is to be continued—living in the present, lingering in the past, and always waiting on the threshold, poised to begin.

THE RED SHOES

When I was eleven I'd accompany my mother
To San Diego State College, where she was taking courses
For some degree or other (she taught reading to kids).
It was summer. Maybe she didn't want to leave me at home,
Or maybe I wanted to come along—I don't remember.
I was into microscopes and blood: I had a compound model
With three lenses I bought at an optical store on the second floor
Of a Chandleresque building with exposed ironwork,
Like the building in *Double Indemnity*. I would read in the
     library—
Edgar Allan Poe and *Great Tales of Terror and the Supernatural*,
Where I first read H. P. Lovecraft ("The Rats in the Walls")—
And wander around the Mediterranean-style campus
With its arcades and red tile roofs, overlooking a valley.
One afternoon I came across some people gathered around the
     corpse
Of a gigantic giraffe sunk in the mud behind the biology building.
It didn't look like something that had once possessed a soul,
But as they did their dissection they let me make a slide of its
     blood,

Which I stained with a Venetian dye so I could look at its cells
Under my microscope, and compare them to those in birds'
    blood, and my own.
The "Kindly Professor," as I came to call him (he was all of
    twenty-five),
Let me come to his class and bring my dinky microscope,
Which he showed to his students and deadpanned, "research
    model,"
As I stood there beaming. The other excitement that summer
Was a movie, *The Red Shoes*, that was showing in a campus
    theater,
An unlikely choice for a boy of eleven who hated the piano
    lessons
His father made him take, so I guess my mother made me go.
I sat there in the dark as the Technicolor dream washed over me
And the gorgeous Moira Shearer danced her way to death,
Borne inexorably aloft by the red shoes through the long ballet
    scene
Towards the oncoming train at the end, when she lay, her
    body
Broken and bloody, begging Marius Goring, "Take off the red
    shoes";
And then I walked intact into the sunlight and a cool arcade.

I didn't start out to write a poem about my mother,
But unchecked memories carry you away, like the shoes
In *The Red Shoes*. I'm sure I loved her then:
She was smart and funny and more down to earth

Than my father, who, when he wasn't somewhere with the
    Navy,
Affected these aesthetic airs and sang too loud in church.
I didn't really mind the trips to the North Park health food
    store,
Where I'd have a carrot shake, or the pile of pills each morning
    by my millet,
Though they prefigured the manias to come: the single-minded
Ferocity tinged with sweetness, the obsessions with nutrition
And religion, the body and the soul, which led from one fad to
    the next
Until her heart gave out, and the doctrines dropped away
And she could fill that vacuum with herself. When she was dying
I was stunned to find myself relieved at how unpleasant she'd
    become,
For it relieved the grief. "When I grow too old to dream /
I'll have you to remember"—I felt my father's sob
As they sang it at the funeral, but then he came into his own
And lived for years and years, his decorating instincts
    unrestrained at last.
I'd visit him each year, and sometimes I'd drive past the college
(Now called a university), which was all new buildings hiding
    the arcades,
The Spanish roofs, the library where I'd whiled the afternoons
    away
While she went to class, if they're still there at all. The past
Is hidden, but never goes away: I'm spending a semester in the
    East

And saw that movie yesterday at Film Forum in New York.
(You didn't think that I remembered those two names
After all these years, did you? But the rest is clear as day,
As clear as yesterday.) They're both dead now,
And all I have to wrestle with are words, and yet these
Syllables bring back the feeling of those summer afternoons,
The red tile roofs, the blood and the ballet, as I sit here in the
    future
I couldn't imagine then, waiting for one I can't imagine now.
Life seems unreal until it suddenly comes back to you,
But by then it's too late—time makes us different people,
Sometimes for better, sometimes, alas, for worse,
But the past is a diversion, and there's nothing you can
Do with it but see it through, and then put it away.
I want to put the memories away, walk out into the cool
Sunlight of a real day, and take off the red shoes.

ALFRED HITCHCOCK

There are four movies that I saw
Between the ages of ten and fourteen that became
Parts of my life, for what that's worth:
The Man Who Knew Too Much, which I saw

When I was ten at the Mission Theatre
On Fifth Avenue, half a block north of the Orpheum.
Doris Day and Jimmy Stewart leave their stylish
London friends completely in the lurch

In their elegant hotel room, and set out in search
Of Ambrose Chapel, which turns out not to be a person,
But rather a church where their kidnapped son is being held.
There's a concert and a clash of cymbals and a shot;

A party at an embassy where she sings "Que Sera,"
While he sneaks up the stairs to find their son.
The suspense becomes unbearable, but it all ends well,
And with their death-defying labors done,

•   •   •

The three of them return at last to their hotel,
Where their friends have fallen fast asleep. *Vertigo*,
Which I'll come back to in a minute, came to the Orpheum
In 1958, followed a year later by *North by Northwest*,

Which is completely captivating—probably the best
Piece of entertainment ever filmed. Cary Grant
Is on the lam, wrongly suspected of an assassination
In a crowded lobby at the United Nations.

He sneaks aboard a train bound for Chicago,
And in the dining car falls in with Eva Marie Saint.
They seem to hit it off, engaging in some quaint
Old-fashioned bantering and flirtation

Before repairing to her sleeping car, where,
Alas, she makes him sleep alone. He has a close call
With a crop duster in a tall cornfield in downstate
Illinois, leaving him covered with dust, yet still impeccable,

And the movie culminates in a scene atop Mt. Rushmore,
Where after clambering around a presidential nostril
Or two he saves her life, and pulls her up into their nuptial bed,
An upper berth back on a train—although the famous phallic
    finish,

As the train goes roaring through a tunnel, went over my head.
I saw *Psycho* at the California Theatre on Fourth in 1960.

It starts out in a seedy hotel room in Phoenix—so much
Grimmer than the hotel room in *The Man Who Knew Too
Much*—

Which foreshadows the seedy Bates Motel. Janet Leigh
Is also on the lam—flight seems to be a reoccurring theme—
And holes up there, and then decides to turn around.
Before she can she's gruesomely dispatched (we later learn)

By Anthony Perkins in the notorious shower scene,
Which tore me out of my seat. He's devoted to his mother,
Who shows up in another scene that made me jump,
As Martin Balsam, a detective fresh from talking to Leigh's lover

John Gavin, heads up the stairs to the mother's bedroom
And she lunges out at him with her brutal knife. She appears
    again
At the movie's climax, when Leigh's sister, Vera Miles, finds her
    in the fruit cellar
And she slowly turns to her, the way a malignant figure in a
    dream,

With an averted face, starts to turn to you, and then you
    scream.
All of these movies were tremendously entertaining, sure,
And a lot of fun, but *Vertigo* was something else again—a pure
Fever dream, a fantasy fulfilled and then at once destroyed.

                    •   •   •

I saw it again last weekend at the Rosebud Cinema in
   Wauwatosa,
And it still retains its power to disturb. It's Jimmy Stewart once
   again,
A wealthy acrophobic retired policeman hired by a college
   friend,
Tom Helmore, to investigate his wife, supposedly possessed by
   the ghost

Of her great-grandmother, Carlotta Valdes, who killed herself
At twenty-six, his wife's own age. Kim Novak impersonates the
   wife
As part of a plot to murder her. Stewart falls in love with her
Of course, but driven forward by Carlotta's furious rage to end
   her life,

Novak leaps (?) from the bell tower of Mission San Juan
   Bautista,
Though it's the real wife who falls. Stewart is destroyed. And
   then his life
Starts to begin again. He meets a shopgirl, Judy (it's Novak
   again),
And tries to resurrect the past, remaking her in the image of his
   dead love

Madeleine, until, his fantasy complete, she stands before him in
   a gauzy haze
—And then Carlotta's necklace makes him see the truth. In a daze

He drives her to the mission where the "suicide" occurred,
And struggling against his vertigo he drags her up into the
  tower

Where—hysterical—she admits to everything. Suddenly a nun
Emerges from the shadows muttering "I heard voices."
Novak screams and plunges to her death. Stewart stands there
  stunned
And silent, looking down in disbelief at what he's done.

STELE

I love the past tense, but you can't live there.
I love the stories you believe add up to you,
Though they never do. I love the way
The rhythms and the tenses and the words
Add up to nothing, or to a diversion, or to this:
I *know* this place, and even think it's true
(If places can be true), but what does it say?
That if I wake I'll wake up into it, and then go on?
Or is it just a state of mind, a place to linger in
Or stay, whose seeming is the whole of its reality?
I was born to indecision: I follow thoughts
Wherever they lead, and dreams until it's clear
They won't come true. I live in my imagination
Most of the time, biding what's left of my time
And waiting for no one in particular to come—
Waiting for an ending endlessly deferred,
When you (the reader of my life) and I are one.

THE POEM OF THE MIND

The poem of the mind starts with a question,
But which one? It fears the "loss of problems"
Wittgenstein feared, it finds its pleasure in the
Trance that suddenly comes over one, the dawning
Of a new romance, the promise offered one last time.
Come here, it seems to say (a plea addressed to no one),
Come with me down this course. No one answers
Of course, because the way is solitary and the end
Uncertain, but it doesn't matter in the end. Like someone
Walking in his sleep who dreams of walking in his sleep,
It gradually becomes the thing that it envisions, simultaneously
Inhabiting and moving towards an unknown destination.
You think you've read it all before, and of course you have,
For the poem of the mind is inexhaustible. It never ends,
As the mind never ends, yet sometimes disappears from view
Before emerging in a new form, one resembling the old form
As one day resembles another, or the mild afternoon light
Resembles that of its first morning, the site of its first illusion.
It treasures its illusions, for they're what it is and where it lives:
Wandering through the gallery of lost illusions, it pauses

Before one or two, before the catastrophe of reality intrudes—
Bone smashed on asphalt, gunshot blowing out the head—
And then continues on. It isn't a question of belief or disbelief,
But of a freedom from belief, an acquiescence in appearance.
To be satisfied with appearance is to be perpetually unsatisfied
A small voice says, and yet its reservation goes unheeded.
Who could actually live that way? *How else?* goes the reply.
I'm just like you, if you don't ask me what that means.
The poem of the mind portrays an almost vacant mind
Whose thoughts remain unfinished, like the unfinished
    paintings
Hanging on the studio wall above the blood-splattered floor.
When does it turn, the way a sonnet turns? When do questions
Take on a grammar of their own, answering themselves
Day after day, until the inwardness becomes as unbearable
As an encroaching blindness? This is what eternal life must be:
To live completely in the present, locked in a self-absorption
So intense its end is unimaginable, where nothing can be real
Outside its own arena of awareness, like the shot it can't hear,
The crash it can't feel. Feelings are supposed to be its heart,
But they're imaginary feelings, based on an imaginary life.
It posits an indifferent life behind the real one, an indifferent
World that wanes and waxes as a whole, yet never really
Changes: happy for a day, and then unhappy on the next,
But what's the difference? Parts are real too, and even
Fragments have to come to something in the end. At length
It starts to settle and subside: the morning light is gradual
In the window, as the contours of a vague presence

That wasn't there before emerge. *Here you are,*
It says to itself. *I'm glad you've finally come home.*
The impulse that engendered its convulsive exercise
Pulls back and takes a breath, recasting its answer
In the form of a new question, as the poem of the mind
Returns at last to its beginning, and is satisfied.

THE WHOLE CREATION

for Harold Bloom

I still believe in it, though I don't know who else does.
I first experienced it in the building I have an office in now
And called it poetry, but the word was just a placeholder
For something undefined, though that's too simple a way to put it.
You aspire to what you admire, whether you understand it
Or not, and now that I've retired into it, I want to remain here
In my home away from home, roaming without sadness
Through the whole creation, through the long song of myself.
Some days I wake up in a room suffused with sunlight
"Like a yellow jelly bean," as Jimmy Schuyler put it
In his great poem "Hymn to Life," but it's not that kind of day.
There was a blizzard overnight, and everything's shut down,
Including my seminar, and so instead of ruminating on that poem
I'm fooling around with this one, and looking out the window at
    the snow.
What *is* poetry anyway? It falls like snow, and settles where it falls,

And melts. I thought I was going to wake up in another world,
And so I have, but it's the one where I began. The sunlight
Just came back, as what begins in gladness and uncertainty
    matures
Into a kind of baffled happiness, unfinished and complete.
I have the sense of something constantly receding, the way
The future does, then suddenly returning, like the past.
It's all so confusing, and yet it doesn't bother me—
Everything evaporates, but some of it eventually comes back
In the uncertain form it assumed in the first place—
A remnant still intact and seemingly as distant from me
As the books in the library I keep remembering and looking up,
And as close as them too. But I loved it, whatever it was.

EGGHEADS

In the fifties people who were smart
And looked smart were called eggheads.
Adlai Stevenson, who was bald and went to Princeton,
Was the quintessential egghead, and so he lost
To Dwight Eisenhower, the president of Columbia.
Dave Brubeck was an egghead, with his horn-rimmed
Glasses and all those albums of jazz at colleges,
Though on NPR last week he claimed he wasn't smart.
I took piano lessons from his brother Howard
In the Thearle Music Building in San Diego in the fifties,
Which probably would have made me an egghead by contagion
If it hadn't been for Sputnik, which made being smart
Fashionable for a while (as long as you didn't look smart).
Beatniks weren't eggheads: eggheads were uptight
And buttoned down, wore black shoes instead of sandals,
And didn't play bongo drums or read poetry in coffeehouses.

What sent me on this memory trip was the realization
That stupidity was in style again, in style with a vengeance—
Not that it was ever out of style, or confined to politics

("We need more show and less tell," wrote an editor of *Poetry*
About a poem of mine that he considered too abstract).
The new stupidity doesn't have a name or a characteristic look,
And it's not just in style, it *is* a style, a style of seeing everything
    as style,
Like Diesel jeans, or glasses and T-shirts, or a way of talking
    on TV:
Art as style, science as a style, and intelligence as a style too,
Perhaps the egghead style without the smarts. It's politics
Where stupidity and style combine to form the perfect storm,
As a host of stylized, earnest airheads emerge from the
    greenrooms
Of the Sunday morning talk shows, mouthing talking points
In chorus, playing their parts with panache and glowing with
    the glow
You get from a fact-free diet, urged on by a diminutive
    senator
Resembling a small, furious gerbil. If consistency is the
    hobgoblin
Of little minds, these minds are enormous, like enormous
    rooms.

It wasn't always like this. Maybe it wasn't much better,
But I used to like politics. I used to like arguing with Paul
    Arnson
On the Luther League bus, whatever it was we argued about.
It was more like a pastime, since if things were only getting
    better

Incrementally, at least they weren't steadily getting worse:

Politicians put their heads together when they had to, Fredric March

And Franchot Tone gave their speeches about democracy and shared values

In *Seven Days in May* and *Advise and Consent*, and we muddled through.

Everett Dirksen, Jacob Javits, Charles Percy—remember them?

They weren't eggheads or Democrats (let alone beatniks), yet they could

Talk to eggheads and Democrats (I'm not sure about beatniks),

And sometimes even agreed with them. It was such an innocent time,

Even if it didn't seem particularly innocent at the time, yet a time

That sowed the seeds of its own undoing. I used to listen to the radio,

Curious as to what the right was on about now, but I'm not curious anymore,

Just apprehensive about the future. I'd rather listen to "Take Five"

Or watch another movie, secure in the remembrance of my own complacency,

The complacency of an age that everyone thought would last forever

—As indeed it has, but only in the imagination of a past that feels fainter

And fainter as I write, more and more distant from a bedroom
    where I lie awake
Remembering Sputnik and piano lessons, bongo drums and
    beatniks, quaint
Old-fashioned Republicans and Democrats and those eggheads
    of yore.

THE GREAT GATSBY

. . . the old island here that flowered once for Dutch sailors'
eyes—a fresh, green breast of the new world.

I've read it dozens of times, starting in high school.
I even listened to it once, on a set of records
I got from the library, sitting in my bedroom by a window
Looking out upon a canyon and a mountain to the east.
The earnest interplay of sentiments and sentences
Propels you forward, past the parties and the beautiful shirts,
The lists, the midtown brightness, towards the moonlight
And the green light and the water waiting for you at the end.
It's like the record of a dream, compelled in equal parts
By personality and history, by public destiny and geography
Played out in private, that each time I'd pretend to share.
I hate comparisons: a thing should be unique, and fill its space.
And yet there's something irresistible about what isn't there,
The beckoning undefined that cloaks itself in metaphors,
The *something else* that waits to take the place of what you have.
It holds the promise of a better life, or at least a different one,

And so I started on my quest, a voyage centered vaguely
On Manhattan, and whatever else that might turn out to mean.
My ticket was an aptitude for SATs. My *Half Moon*
Was a Greyhound bus that found a passage to the east.

The things you seek are never those you find. As one
Supplants the other each remains unreal and unexplored,
And yet the bare geography is still the same. The passage west
Became a fresh, terrestrial paradise, and then a state of mind,
Though on the ordinary maps they coincide—the meadows
That were Harlem, and the forests that became Times Square;
The place where Sneden's Landing turned into a song.
What started out as commerce gradually became the old idea
Of a new form of grace, a prolonged "capacity for wonder,"
Then for something harder to define. The commercial venture
Petered out somewhere near Albany. The space it opened up
Stayed open through the four succeeding centuries, altered
Into something no one on the ship could even recognize.
The next voyage failed too. The Northwest Passage
Was a myth, though an essential one, a kind of catalyst.
The ship of state "had somewhere to get to and sailed calmly on"
—Distracted now and then by revisions and upheavals—
Towards a mysterious destination that continues to recede,
While Hudson and his son and a remnant of his crew,
Set adrift in a small boat, vanished from history.

Sometimes I wonder what I'm doing here, in a reduced
Midwest, amid what's left of the "thrilling returning

Trains" of the Milwaukee Road, listening to Mabel Mercer

Singing "Did You Ever Cross Over to Sneden's?"

And reading *Gatsby* one more time. What I had in mind

When I set out from San Diego on that bus had as much to do

With the real world as Tomorrowland did with the real future,

Which is where I find myself today. In the art museum's
    basement

There's a Thomas Cole landscape of a mountain in a storm,

Ablaze in the imaginary wilderness that ended centuries before.

What starts in wonder and a promise settles into a hope

That springs eternal, and then into disappointment, as the end

Becomes so grandiose and undefined there's nothing there to see.

That's the trouble with the sublime: it feels so full of purpose

At the outset, yet as time goes by it comes to seem beside the
    point,

Like a dream I'd only wished I had. Who cares if it came
    true—

And even if it did, how would I know? I'd have felt the same,

No matter what I'd started out to do, and in any case, as Gatsby
    said,

It was just personal. And when I try to think of what it meant,

I can't remember—it was all so long ago, and it was new.

ROTC KILLS

for Fabrizio Mondadori

I'm retired, I'm sitting in a house I made
In my imagination years ago, that now is real.
On the walls are posters from the Harvard
Strike in 1969 I saved for their designs
And then forgot about, and now they're here:
STOP HARVARD EXPANSION, STRIKE
FOR THE 8 DEMANDS, and then the best of all,
In tiny red letters with three red bayonets,
ROTC KILLS (pronounced *rot-cee kills*). From here inside
Time seems unreal, I'm back in graduate school,
But then the mind ascends and time becomes objective,
I'm myself again, at home again, and sixty-four.
The particulars of a life, the pattern of a life:
These are the poles the mind, in the guise of a poem,
Floats back and forth between. The calm elation,
The deflating sigh: the trees are tossing in the wind, the leaves

Unfurl their silvery undersides, the soft clouds drift across the sky.
Time may be an abstraction, but it makes the days go by,
The days I never thought I'd see, when the music of the sixties
Lost its way, became too faint to hear, the voices fell away,
And then it all came down to *me*. What *were* those eight
    demands?
I can't recall to save my life. I lived there, I breathed that air,
And sometimes some of it drifts back to me. "You should
    join PL,"
Paul said as we were sitting in the lounge. Picketing
The GE plant in Lynn didn't much appeal to me, so I just
Said it seemed too hard to square with being married
And finishing my degree. "Yes! That's what's so great about it!"
He replied, as I rolled my eyes. Or Jonny Supak's plan
To hold the chairman (Rogers Albritton) hostage in his office:
"The kids are stealing underwear from Filene's Basement,
Asking for the Red Army! 'Where's the Red Army?' they're
    asking!"
It felt so all-important at the time, in a surreal way, the endless
Back-and-forths, the forums, teach-ins, meetings and analyses,
    strategic
Planning sessions ("But—but that would be *capitulationism*!"),
And look at what it came to. I didn't even vote in 1968
(Chicago was too fresh), but on election night I found myself
Nostalgic for the Hump, only by then it was too late.
It's nice to think it might have made a difference,
But that's just wishful thinking: money finds a way,
And if it wasn't Nixon . . . Too much has gone

To be restored, and as for money = speech, it's a joke:
The silence in what people used to call the streets
Is deafening, all talk is on the radio, as money
Quietly wraps its hands around the country's throat.

I wonder what Larry, my general contractor, Jeff,
My carpenter, Jerry, who (occasionally) did the plumbing,
Made of all the posters. They couldn't be more friendly,
But Wisconsin's a peculiar state—La Follettes vs.
Tail-Gunner Joe, the sewer socialist mayors of Milwaukee
And the park where Hitler lovers rallied. I'm not sure
I could explain them in a way they'd understand
("See, there were these demands"), but then there's Mitch,
The landscape guy, whose countercultural compulsion to
     explain
Is straight from Paul and Jonny. It's beautiful out here,
I feel alive and out of it, from the aisles of the Piggly Wiggly,
The World of Variety, to the steps of the Unique Café,
The shelves of Gasser Hardware. Driving through "the vast
Obscurity beyond the city," it suddenly seems so clear,
Though the clarity is probably deceptive, as clarity often is:
Beyond the signs for prefab homes (I bought one),
Pro-life billboards with a baby floating in what looks like
Amniotic fluid ("Before I formed you in the womb I knew
     you"),
Madmen on the radio denouncing Baptists and Freemasons,
Lie the streams, the rivers, the steep, unglaciated hills.
You couldn't climb them (would you want to?),

But it's comforting to know they're there. We live in different
Dreamworlds, wandering through a wilderness of words,
While the real story writes itself in silence. It's forty years ago,
It's yesterday, and when I try to think of what those posters
    represent
I realize they're footnotes, surface irritants that left the
    underlying
Language undisturbed. Their meaning is the interval between
    the times
Of then and now, the times of looking forward and of drifting
    back.
"They flash upon that inward eye," and then they're gone,
I'm sitting in a room, I'm looking at the trees, unsure if this is
Something other than another version of *The Big Chill*,
A movie I despise. I hope it is. I saw Paul not too long ago—
He's mellowed, everyone has mellowed, "mellow"
Is a word for disappointed. The sixties had their charms
But patience and contentment weren't among them.
It was a brief, imaginary time, swept along by anthems
And guitar heroes, when tomorrow had arrived,
The air was filled with specious possibilities,
All the demands were just, the kids kept calling
For the Red Army, and rotc killed.

LIKE GODS

The philosopher David Lewis spun a fantasy of two omniscient gods who know about one world, which might as well be ours. Each knows precisely all there is to know, the grand "totality of facts, not things." Each knows the pattern of the light on each neglected leaf millennia ago. Each knows the number of the stars, their ages, all the distances between them, all the "things too tiny to be remembered in recorded history—the backfiring of a bus in a Paris street in 1932," as well as all the things that history distorts or just can't see, like the thought that must have flashed across Patroklos's mind (if he'd existed and had had a mind—the middle knowledge of the schoolmen) when Hektor split his stomach with a spear (if he'd existed too). Each one looks on, as though through ordinary eyes, as "Mme Swann's enormous coachman, supervised by a groom no bigger than his fist and as infantile as St. George, endeavoured to curb the ardour of the quivering steel-tipped pinions with which they thundered over the ground," and sees "the grey 'toppers' of old" the gentlemen strolling with her wore, the little "woollen cap from which stuck out two blade-like partridge feathers" that she wore (or would have worn if they and she'd been real). Each monitors the photons through the slits, the slow decay of radium, and knows the ratio of vermouth to gin in someone's first martini at Larre's. Each knows what Darragh, Geoff, and Willy knew before the bullet or the pavement killed their worlds, and where the shots came from in Dallas. Each knows precisely what the other knows, in all the senses of those words, and if a question has a factual answer, each can answer it. Yet there's a question neither can resolve: Which god am I?

The question posits both a world and a unique perspective on that world, which neither has. And if gods One and Two could reify themselves by wondering who or what they were, they'd have to know the answer—and, because they don't, they can't. Could gods like those be real, in something like the sense that you and I are real? But then, what sense is that? Gods One and Two are you and I writ large: I wander out into the day and feel the sunlight on my face. I see the sunlight on the first spring leaves like green foam on the trees, and so do you. The world we have in common, that the gods can comprehend in its entirety, remains beyond my grasp, and yours. The world I know belongs entirely to me, as yours belongs entirely to you. I know my world completely, as the gods know ours, because it's nothing but my take on things, and starts and ends with me. I'm both the author and the captive of my world, because my take on things is all there is to me. When Mary, in Frank Jackson's philosophical diversion, wanders from her room of black and white and shades of gray and finally sees a rose, and then goes on in sunlight, into the Hofgarten, and drinks coffee, and talks for hours, it's hard to see how all of *this* (as she might say) could be an artifact of her perspective. But it is.

So what? Philosophers tell stories, but they make them up, and what are they to me? Sometimes I think I'm humoring myself (a good thing I suppose) with an extended exercise in nonsense. *Have breakfast, have a cup of strong black common sense, get over it*, I tell myself, refuting Berkeley with my foot. Instead of this entanglement of self with self, why can't I just relax into my place inside the natural order, be a thing within the solid scheme of things, a Dane in Denmark? How can fantasies, unreal by definition, show me what I am, and know? How can the poetry of possibilities dissolve the prose of facts? My little life sustains me while it can, and that's enough. It may be all contingent, but it's real, and when catastrophes occur, as they inevitably do, I'd rather they occur to *me*, instead of writing them away, or redefining happiness or sorrow or tranquillity as alterations of some abstract point of view that points at nothing. Inescapable illusions must be real, or might as well be real, no matter where reflection on them leads; and if accepting them means taking things on faith, that's fine. Who wants to be a posit, or a site of possibilities? Who wants to walk out and evaporate into this green spring day? Who wants to have sex with a wraith?

No matter where reflection on them leads. It leads, of course, to me. A cri de coeur is not an argument, but where the real argument begins. Hopkins: "searching nature I taste *self* at one tankard, that of my own being." Kant: "a feeling of an existence without the least concept," meaning that despite the certainty I have, I've no idea what I really am, or where, and as for "searching nature," I have no idea even where to start. These matters mean the world to me, and yet no matter how I try to come to grips with them, they slip away. *I* and *here* and *now* are ever present, yet they vanish in the act of apprehension, as a poem turns into language as you write it down. Dimensionless, atemporal, imprisoned in the present—even as I say them to myself the words fall short of what I thought I started out to say, like the conclusion of an argument too close to me to share, or like an empty thought balloon that hangs above me in the air. It's not the question of what makes me who I am through time—of how a figure in a photograph from 1985, a couple sitting in the garden of the small Hôtel des Marronniers just off the rue Jacob, could be the person who remembers her and thinks of him today—but of what constitutes me now, and of what made me then. If giving it a name won't help, then neither will pretending it's divine. If I should be supplanted by a bright recording angel knowing everything about me in the way the gods know all about their world, I wouldn't have survived. She takes the whole thing in—the house on Maxim Street, the bike rides down the hill on Wabash Street, my high school friends, their friends, the friends of friends of friends—with eyes that monitor my back, my face, the traces in my brain projected on a screen, the n degrees of separation linking me to nearly everyone who's ever lived, a thing within a wilderness of things, with each one locked inside a universe with no outside, of which there's nothing she can see.

How could it be an afterlife? It's just a different life, another life, complete or incomplete as anyone's, consumed by questions that elude it, not because she can't remember, but because the words that make them up are undefined: Which one of them was I? Which world was mine?

LOCUS SOLUS

I'm a sucker for the private place,
Though it's boring once you've found it:
You're always right, which makes being right
Worthless, and yet you want to stay there
Even though you hate it. I remember
The initial vision: elegance
Mingled with the ordinary, intimacy
In a kingdom of three or four. Ecstasy
Was a dream before it was a drug,
However oversold. I miss the distractions
That distracted me—distracted me
From what exactly? From anonymity
And inconsequence, and from how tenuous
Life feels when you're alone and nobody cares
What's true or false? The elegance
Is always in the telling, not in the truth, and yet
Sometimes the words still speak to me
As if they were true. They stick in my mind,
They stick in my throat. It's still there.

THE SPECIOUS PRESENT

. . . he lives eternally who lives in the present.

Wittgenstein

I live, as you do, to celebrate myself,
But it isn't easy. Sometimes life goes well
And brings a sudden sense of exaltation
That doesn't last, and quickly seems beside the point,
As meaningless to me as someone else's happiness.
I have to fill each moment with my *self*, whatever *that* is,
Living in what someone called "the specious present"
And slowly approaching the end of what I think of as my life,
Though it's really no one's life. I try to see it as a sign
Of the soul at the center of a story taking place
Almost entirely in my own imagination,
But it's all fake. The *I* that stares out through my eyes
Isn't the same as yesterday's or tomorrow's *I*,
A virtual, transitory thing without a permanent existence,

Or even an intermittent one, broken up by sleep,
That springs to life each day and wears its moment like a shell.
The moments form a sequence, A or B, like a chain of way
    stations
Stretching out before and after this one, each as empty
As an empty sky, drained of my presence. Isn't there another
Form of exhilaration, one that feels almost like resignation
At the way time flies? I look forward to a future
With more time to travel, and grandchildren would be nice
Sometime before the inevitable, though it won't be me
Who gets to see them, or me who dies.

SELF-PORTRAIT ON YOUTUBE

His reasoning was specious, and did much to reassure me.

P. G. Wodehouse

Like a casement opening out upon a world
He chooses not to see, the prisoner of a point of view
Remains complacent in that choice, until a slight
Alteration of perspective, a trick of light, reveals a small
Illuminated window in a corner of the factory's dull façade.
I don't like looking at myself (*I like to watch myself*,
Says the countervoice)—how can that odd, uncomprehending
Object looming right in front of me be *me* (*and there I am*)?
I was wandering through the Internet last week
(As if I'd nothing better to do) in a dilatory state of mind,
Revisiting my usual sites, checking my e-mail now and then
For news of something interesting or new or strange,
And then I came across myself. I was standing at a podium
In a bookstore, reciting a poem I wrote last summer

About the sixties, about how the world you believed you knew

Changes in ways you couldn't have foreseen; about
   disappointment.

It all seemed tentative, yet tentative in a way I wanted it
   to be,

For thought itself is tentative. As the reader plodded along

A sense of peace came over me, as though the person I was
   watching

Were the real me, relieved of the burdens of self-consciousness

And spelling out the words as I had meant them all along.
   Perhaps

Life *is* best looked at from a single window (I saw *Gatz* last
   week too,

Another objectification of self-consciousness, of perfect
   sentences),

But a perspective boxes you in. To see yourself the way others
   see you

Is a wonderful kind of freedom, the freedom of starting over
   again

Without preconceptions, the freedom of looking at your
   heart.

I'm at the age when death becomes a fact, however long
   deferred,

Instead of just an abstract possibility, which is why I crave
   distractions.

The mirror is too intimate. What I want is the cool
   detachment

Of another person's vantage point, free from the distorting

Self-conceptions consciousness imposes on itself, when the
   mind
Is caught in the brief interval between thought and action
And it finds a way of moving forward, and it's time to start.
   .

THE EMERGENCE OF THE HUMAN

You can watch it as you walk through the Uffizi:
Gold leaf, egg tempera, gold halos on the flat saints
And on the flat Madonna and detached bambino
Balanced precariously on her lap, her eyes to one side.
The composition is meant to look like something you can't see,
To illuminate a mystery. Yet now and then some vaguely
Contoured hills replace the gold, a figure seems to look at you
Or look like someone from the artist's town, or the baby's
Features soften into the faint suggestion of a smile.
The impulse is always towards the truth, the only question is
The kind of truth: iconic or demystified, a representation of the
    word
Or the word made flesh. Siena's figures floated on the surface,
Shorn of their misgivings and desires, while somewhere down the
    road
Something was happening of which Siena didn't have a clue.
You can see it happen in the landscapes in the background,
Drifting from nowhere in particular into those bluish
Mountains harboring the caves I saw last week; in Christ's
Contorted features made of paint that feels like flesh,

That yields a massive Holy Family without halos;
In the reinvention of mythology, and then within mythology,
The shift from Venus chaste and balanced in the foam,
Caressed by winds, to Venus lying on a bed with a small dog at
    her feet,
A "nude woman" who stares at you indifferently and reeks
    of sex.
And then the floodgates open and the world comes rushing in:
The "crude, expressive naturalism" of Caravaggio and his
    followers—
Medusa on a shield, screaming from her mouth's black hole,
And then a real Cardinal, palpably corrupt, and Bacchus
As a smirking peasant boy, his upper body glistening with
    sweat,
And then a blood-soaked dental scene of overwhelming cruelty,
    then a thug;
All hanging in an exhibition in the Pitti Palace just across the
    bridge.
"And I am sweating a lot by now" as I make my way along Via
    Romana,
Following this trajectory—a trajectory that started with a
    mystery
And peeled away its layers to reveal the human form inside—
To its logical conclusion in La Specola, the anatomical museum
Filled with specimens of almost every living thing,
And then the finally human body, open for the world to see,
Like David flayed, or St. Sebastian disemboweled
Instead of punctured here and there by arrows, and brains

Where golden halos used to be. Somewhere in the remote past
There was a message from an angel. What happened next
Depends on whom you ask, but if you ask me, I'd say it led to
    these—
These wax models of the body, with its veins, entrails, and
    nerves,
From which nothing is missing except its old significance;
As though the history of art were the story of its disappearance,
Of the deflation of the word into a slowly disappearing
Word made flesh, of the flesh demystified at last.

BURNISHED DAYS

I came back at last to my own house.

I went for a walk this afternoon,
Down Mercer Street, past the Seminary
And out to the Graduate College, revisiting
The world where I began to feel like this
And sound this way. I clambered up the carillon
To see the local world, and wandered through the arch
Where Willy used to hear his family's voices.
We like to think that we're the logical conclusion
Of what we knew, and the choices we made,
But it isn't true. I think "But it isn't true"
Should be my motto, or the fortune in my cookie,
For whatever the book of the past contains
I don't know how to read it. The certainties of a day
Give way to second thoughts and doubts, and questions
Come quickly, to which the answers take their time.
The January sun was filtering through the trees
As I walked back home, subdued by the second sight
Of bare branches intertwined with evergreens and yellow
Sunlight on the towers, as the light declined.

ARTHUR

You go to school, and stay there all your life.
You study who you are, and you remain that way
The rest of your life. Language is real,
Consciousness is real, and poetry a way of making
The unreal real. Desire is unsatisfied desire,
Or you'd never feel it, and the mind you try to study
Is your own mind, once removed. In winter
I came back to where I started, and when spring
   exploded
Into blossoms and leaves, I felt myself the same
As when I started—like a traveler who, his journey done,
Feels himself once more at home, and can't move.
It's not a matter of remembering who you are,
But of staying there, as years go by and people change
Or seem to change. It's not a matter of belief, but
   of feeling,
And if you know that all those feelings can't be true,
So much the worse for knowledge. I knew that home,
When you come back to it, feels smaller, but I'd forgotten
How the mind expands to fill it, turning into language

As the consonants dissolve and the vowels run into colors
Like flowers frosting the trees, the brilliant blues and greens
Of an afternoon in college, listening to nothing but itself.

You don't know what I'm saying, do you? I'll be explicit:
Time kills you, while places stay essentially the same.
Time annihilates you, for what you think and see and feel
Is what you are, with nothing at the center to sustain it
But the continuity that consciousness and memory provide.
You're new each day, while places have their stuff and structure
To sustain them, so that coming home at last feels like
A logical conclusion to a life, although there's no one there.
I know that something like this must be true, and yet
Life doesn't feel that way. It feels like something hiding
In the years and reemerging when the stars are in alignment
Or a certain slant of sunlight reappears. I leave my office,
Passing by the lecture hall where forty-seven years ago
I took a course on Plato, down the stairs and out into the
    sunlight
Of an April afternoon, as though I'd never been away. The
    towering,
Transparent sky presides indifferently above it all. I make my
Way through arches, past the sundial and the chapel and the
    library,
To a parking lot, a shopping mall, and then down Ewing Street

To a small grove of trees, where a small man sits and waits.
The towering, transparent sky presides indifferently above it all,

While down below a mind fits in its hollow, as the stories
Flare and flicker in a consciousness of ninety-four:
A sausage in an icebox; Quine, a college president, a dog;
Scoon and Stace and Ledger Wood—I've heard them all before,
Just after Plato and as long ago as half of Arthur's age,
But the wonder is to hear them one last time, with difficulty,
As the syllables wind their way across the afternoon
As across a page. I saw the Mourners at the Met
Last Saturday, two lines of tiny figures frozen as they move
Across a gallery, like minor moments turned to stone,
Or time made tangible. Concealed in its body,
Another person's soul can look more real than your own,
Dissolving as it does into those plans and memories
You have to wander through alone, existing intermittently
In someone else's thoughts, as Arthur does in mine.
The body is a picture of the soul: as it shifts in the shade
And the day begins to wane, it's time to go home.
What started out as years turned into months,
Then weeks, then days, and then a few brief hours
Waiting on a mind neither here nor there nor anywhere,
But that somehow continues to exist, frozen in time
And sitting in a fading light, in an eternal now.

1135

No one has to write any special way—
You make it up as you go along. I started
Writing this way—no thoughts at first,
Then a lot of words in the guise of thoughts,
Then real thoughts—a long time ago.
You can write or think about death directly,
Or you can write about it by indirection
And delay, the way the diary of a day
Reflects the silence waiting darkly at the end,
Like the silence lingering after graduation,
When the students have all gone away
And the ghost campus descends.
I don't know what to say about Darragh—
A painter who gradually convinced himself
That he saw what he didn't actually see,
Until finally he couldn't see at all. I loved him
In a way, though the "in a way" tells all:
There was something not quite there, and now
There's nothing there at all. I drove by his house
Last Saturday, when I was visiting Bob.

Vines and weeds were everywhere, bushes
Encroached upon the porch, there was a dull,
Uneasy feeling something bad had happened there
That left an empty house with empty windows
I had to stretch to see through, staring into rooms as
Empty as a skull from which the mind has gone.
I couldn't look in the studio. I took pictures
Of the For Sale sign, and then drove home
Or what felt like home. The Saturday afternoon
Was bland and beautiful, with no sense of an ending
Or the thought that gradually insinuates itself
In the back of the mind, in a studio, alone.

DREAMS AT SIXTY-FIVE

And the future is still an immense, open dream.

At thirty-six the word's a synonym for something else:
For something you once had, or had and lost, or something
That you hope you're going to have one day; for life's
Exasperating insufficiencies; for anything but real dreams.
I used to love the word, but I detest it now. I became
    addicted
To its sound, its sense or lack of sense, its way of meaning
Anything you wanted it to mean, or wanted to suggest
But couldn't actually describe: a small, immaculate apartment
In the city; a house with chimneys and a yard; a quiet park
At twilight on a summer evening; a lake. In my mind
I'd arrange these things into a sentimental illusion of a future
That's always open, in the sense of never actually arriving,
Or of being unrecognizable when it does—that kind
    of dream,
The kind you make from whatever might come true, and never
    does.

．　．　．

At five I discovered real dreams. After my father came home
From Korea—the USS *Benevolence* sank in San Francisco
    harbor
On his way back, and we listened on the radio for hours as he
    floated there
Before the rescue—we'd go to a drive-in after dinner. My sister
    and I
Put on our pajamas just in case we fell asleep (we always did),
Piled into the car, and with the speaker hanging from the
    driver's window
And bundled up in blankets in the backseat, let the
    picture flow.
I don't remember what the movies were (I remember *Raintree
    County*,
But that was years later) (early memories are like snapshots,
Rather than a cinematic flow) but what I do remember is a
    night at home,
Alone, asleep in bed. I saw—or for the first time dreamed I
    saw—
A tall man in a top hat, with a toilet where his head
    should be
And smoke rings blowing from his spigot of a mouth. I saw a
    fireplace
With blue glass instead of flames, inscribed with someone's
    name
In a small gold script. There was more of course, but that's all I
    remember

After almost sixty years. I told my mother, who explained I'd
  had a dream.
I came to think of dreams as movies in my head, but better
  than the movies at the drive-in:
I could see them every night, and they were mine alone, and
  they were free.

At sixty-five they're neither the romantic fallacies of early
  middle age,
Nor the inner drive-in of my childhood, yet I still love my
  dreams,
Unpleasant though they often are: going somewhere you never
  get to,
Trying unsuccessfully to tie your tie, or button your shirt, or
  completely unprepared
For the examination. The future is still open—as Aristotle
  insisted, that's its nature—
But not open to much, and I still cherish the nocturnal
  entertainments dreams provide.
I started a new diet and stopped drinking for a while, which
  unleashed a torrent of new dreams,
Frenetic, frantic, filled with desperation. I kept trying to shout
At someone that I knew (though now I can't remember who),
  but couldn't shout,
Until I could: *What are you doing? Why are you doing this to
  me?*
*Don't you know how wrong it is, how much it hurts? What do
  you think you're doing?*

Then I woke. Perhaps I should have been disturbed, and yet I
    wasn't—
There was something reassuring in that simulacrum of
    despair
That left me with a kind of peace. They used to think that
    dreams
Revealed a hidden soul, or what you want or fear. I think they're
    brainwork,
Flushing out the synapses and cells of all the stale detritus of
    the day,
The detritus of a lifetime, leaving them replenished and
    refreshed
For whatever happens next. My tendency, as you've observed
    by now,
Is to digress, which is all that dreams can do: no matter how
    unclear
Or how upsetting they might be, they do their job, the job of
Sweeping you away from tedium and care, of filling in the void,
Relieving what would be another ordinary, uneventful day
With brief and meaningless diversions from the here and now.

STARDUST

My father had been a concert violinist
Until WWII, and there was music in his blood—
Not the fluff of popular songs or the travesty
Of rock and roll, but music of high seriousness
And classical intent (though I once elicited a small
Humph! of appreciation when I made him listen
To Fats Domino's "Blueberry Hill" on the car radio)—
And so I had to take piano lessons for seven years
From a wide variety of teachers, though I had no actual
Aptitude for the instrument at all. I began with nuns,
Including Sister Rita Joseph, moved on to Howard Brubeck
In the Thearle Music Building—Dave Brubeck's brother,
Whom he seemed to resent—and then to a man whose name
I can't remember, who lived in a small house surrounded
By castor bean plants, where I once found a turd in the toilet,
And finally ended up with Mr. Ross, an "elderly" (fifty?)
Dirty Old Man, who'd crowd me on the piano bench
And put a hand on my knee as I'd slide farther and farther
Towards the bass end of the keyboard, until I fell off.
He was harmless, though I'd note that none of the nuns

Came on to me, nor any of my other teachers. Two things
Saved me: science, something I was actually good at,
So that when I won the Greater San Diego Science Fair
My father finally realized that my spare time might be better
Spent than in a doomed assault on the piano, and relented;
And the clarinet, an ignoble instrument for which I had a flair.
And so began my meteoric rise up through the ranks
Of the Cody Marching Band and the Woodrow Wilson
Junior High School Orchestra, culminating in a solo
At the annual Parents' Concert, when the perverse
Thought of a spectacularly comic fuckup so took hold
Of my imagination that I finally burst out laughing,
Blowing the entire clarinet—the reed, the mouthpiece,
The whole kit and caboodle—completely out of my mouth,
An inglorious conclusion to my public musical career.

It wasn't my true career. I found the sheet music for "Stardust"
In the piano bench, though what it was doing there remains
A mystery to me—it didn't seem like my father's thing, unless
    he was
A closet sentimentalist, and certainly not my mother's or sister's.
Yet I could play it on the clarinet in a way that made your heart
    break,
As my fingers found the keys that made its melancholy melody
Slide seamlessly from note to note, memory to memory,
Until it reached the end, and hung there for a while in the air.
That melody continues to haunt my adolescent reveries,
Even though I'm sixty-five. Sometimes I wonder why I spend

The lonely nights remembering, but it's a dumb question—
Memory is involuntary, like what we think of as "our" lives:
Most of the future isn't even up to us, and when at last
We discover ourselves, it's usually by default. It turned out
I wasn't as great at science as I'd thought, and now I'm
Left with this. There was always music in my soul,
Yet it was only rock and roll, plus a few tunes
I'd learned to tootle on my clarinet. But as a pianist
I was a bust—I could never find the right keys,
And though eventually I banged out an approximation
Of *Polonaise Militaire*, Mr. Ross had to have fudged
The test that certified that achievement—a complete bust.
But boy could I play "Stardust" on the clarinet.

THE BEAN HOUSE

. . . humming in the summer haze.

Diane christened it the Bean House,
Since everything in it came straight from an
L.L.Bean Home catalog. It looks out upon two
Meadows separated by a stand of trees, and at night,
When the heat begins to dissipate and the stars
Become visible in the uncontaminated sky,
I like to sit here on the deck, listening to the music
Wafting from the inside through the sliding patio doors,
Listening to the music in my head. It's what I do:
The days go by, the days remain the same, dwindling
Down to a precious few as I try to write my name
In the book of passing days, the book of water. Some
Days I go fishing, usually unsuccessfully, casting
Gently across a small stream that flows along beneath
Some overhanging trees or through a field of cows.
Call it late bucolic: this morning I awoke to rain
And a late spring chill, with water dripping from the

Eaves, the apple trees, the pergola down the hill.
No fishing today, as I await the summation
Of my interrupted eclogue, waiting on the rain
And rhythms of the world for the music to resume,
As indeed it does: all things end eventually,
No matter how permanent they seem, no matter how
Desperately you want them to remain. And now the sun
Comes out once more, and life becomes sweet again,
Sweet and familiar, on the verge of summer.

IN THE EMERGENCY ROOM

Like an Edward Hopper painting
Of the future—not one with shadows
Where death hides, but one bathed
In a uniform light, reducing everything,
Human and inanimate alike, to the same size.
Listening in the lobby for my name,
A minute lasts forever—the same minute
Held forever, the minute of a lifetime.
Inside the rooms the nurses come and go,
Illuminated by the fluorescent glow
From the hall, called by a chime. 2:00 a.m.,

Then 3:00. I watch the clock on the wall
Indifferently, dressed in a flimsy gown,
Distracted from whatever brought me here
By drugs, resting in a soft atmosphere
Of humidity and subdued sounds.
The minute hand goes around the clockface
One more time, disclosing nothing new
Beyond a slowly deepening pleasure

Not of my choosing—a vague contentment
That's enough for me now, as I lie here
In a nest of clamps and tubes and bruises,
Perambulating in a light daze of associations
Through other hospitals, other poems,

Other rooms: the dentist's waiting room
In Worcester, Massachusetts, February
Fifth, 1918, where Elizabeth Bishop's
Identity dissolved as the room gave way,
"Sliding beneath a big black wave";
A "dreary little hospital" in Mastic Beach,
Long Island, where Frank O'Hara lay
"In a bed that looked like a large crib," purple
Where the skin showed through the gown,
Stitched together with dark blue thread,
His eyelids bluish black, a tube in one nostril,
Quivering in the crib "like a shaped wound";
Or under ether in the operating room,
When the sound stops and "the mind is
Conscious but conscious of nothing."

Then it breaks. "Are you ready to go home?"
5:00 a.m. Outside the streets are deserted,
There's a huge white winter moon.
I wander around looking for my car,
Forget to turn on the headlights,
But I'm only three blocks from home.

We see death as an extremity, and the line
Between existence and annihilation
As bright and well defined, though it's not.
I suppose that when the time comes,
The first and last time, one crosses it gently—
At least that's the thought, or half thought,
Occupying my mind as I lie here
In the warmth of my bedroom—that,
And a sense of life as something fragile
And ordinary. Thud of a newspaper
Tossed in the dark. Blood on the moon.

BOOK X

In the last book of the *Republic* Plato turns to poetry, implicitly contrasts it with philosophy, and argues that it shouldn't even exist in the ideal city he's meticulously constructed. His reasoning is liable to strike us now as quaint: poets traffic in appearances, not essences, and write of things they don't know anything about, like military strategy and battles; they portray heroic figures in the grip of powerful, deranged emotions, to which their readers must inevitably succumb; and there's a metaphysical complaint: all art, including poetry, is essentially mimetic, and representations are inherently inferior to what they represent. You need to make some changes if you want to know what's going on. Poetry for Plato wasn't what you'd probably think of if you're reading this, a marginalized enactment of experience and subjectivity in which the medium itself is half the point. Nor was philosophy the systematic study of the possibility of meaning we've become accustomed to, but sought instead to penetrate the veil of appearances, arriving at a vision of the good that shows us how we ought to try to live. It's been suggested that to understand him, think of movies and TV instead of poetry, for they're what occupy the space that poetry occupied in Athens. I agree, but then the question ultimately becomes: Should how we try to live be based on fantasies and feelings, or known facts and reason? And the suspicion that the latter aren't much fun shows just how troubling the question really is.

Yet even in their late, attenuated forms philosophy and poetry pose a problem, Plato's problem. *Write what you know:* an admonition that concedes the point that poets usually don't. And what exactly does one know, in the intended sense? I guess what's meant is something like a lived identity within a social world, and yet behind those limited identities lies something larger, something commonplace and ordinary, but at the same time utterly unique. Like the hedgehog, each of us knows just one big thing, a thing philosophy can't capture and that poetry can at best remind us of or intimate, but can't describe. As it extends itself in time the individual life remains a captive of its point of view, confined to what it knows, cut off from all those others that resemble it in all respects but one. It's what I know and everything I know, it's something that I know so thoroughly I can't imagine or describe it, though it fills my eyes. But there's no need for imagery or words: you know it too, for it lies floating in your eyes. Would Plato even recognize a poetry of consciousness? And what of consciousness itself? It's sometimes said to have a history, a recent one, and to have been unknown to Homer's Greeks. But that's a fallacy, inferring how you feel from what you write; moreover, Bernard Williams showed that what they wrote shows that they felt like us. And yet the poems of the articulated consciousness lay in the blank, unwritten future, poised to spring from Hamlet's mind, not Oedipus's; and their challenge to Book X was still to be imagined, still to come.

"There's the part where you say it, and the part where you take it back" (J. L. Austin). I say these things because I want to, and sometimes even think they're true; but now I want to take them back. Knowledge is factive, meaning one can't know what isn't true, and truth is simply correspondence with the facts. What are the facts of consciousness? They're all analogies and metaphors, a feeling of existence but without reality's defining contours, like a sense of something hesitating on the brink of being said, or hiding in the shadows of an inner room. They're all appearances, but appearances of what? Something that wanders up your limbs and nerves and blossoms in your brain? They're all just figments of perspective, of a point of view from which the time is always now, the place is always here, and the thought of something hiding underneath the surface a seductive spell. The harder I try to pin them down the more elusive they become, as gradually the shadows disappear, the words turn into syllables, the face becomes anonymous and leaves me staring at a silver sheet of glass. What starts out as self-scrutiny becomes a study in self-pity, and instead of something tangible and true one winds up chasing the chimeras of Book X: the fruitless quarrel between philosophy and poetry, reason and unreason, and that tedious myth about the soul, of what becomes of it at death, then of its journey and rebirth. I'm tired, I'm far from home, I'm waiting in a chamber in a castle on a mountaintop in Umbria (poets get to do this), seven hundred miles from Athens as the crow flies, where perhaps "the sun still shines upon the hills and has not yet set." I write the way I do because I want it to exist, but then the spell breaks and it dries up like a dream, leaving me with just this smooth, unvariegated surface, which remains.

"His words made us ashamed, and we checked our tears. He walked around, and when he said his legs were heavy he lay on his back as he had been told to do, and the man who had given him the poison touched his body, and after a while tested his feet and legs, pressed hard upon his foot and asked him if he felt this, and Socrates said no. Then he pressed his calves, and made his way up his body and showed us that it was cold and stiff. He felt it himself and said that when the cold reached the heart he would be gone. As his belly was getting cold Socrates uncovered his head—he had covered it—and said—these were his last words—'Crito, we owe a cock to Asclepius; make this offering to him and do not forget.'—'It shall be done,' said Crito, 'tell us if there is anything else.' But there was no answer. Shortly afterwards Socrates made a movement; the man uncovered him and his eyes were fixed. Seeing this Crito closed his mouth and his eyes."

WATCHFUL WAITING

Let's see what happens.

I'm waiting at the bar at Gene's, a place
On West Eleventh Street, just down the street
From the Larchmont Hotel, where I usually stay
When I'm in New York. I come to New York a lot
Since I've retired (from what? someone asked).
Gene's is down some stairs, and sitting at the bar
You can watch people walking by through a window
Above your head, the way I'd imagined New York
When I was a kid, or imagine Dawn Powell's New York.
I sometimes think of life as a vicarious attempt
To make sense of yourself, balancing what you did
And didn't do so that they'll come out even at the end;
And then I think that's probably a waste of time.
It's not a book at all: there's too much time,
And then it's gone; that sense of something waiting
To unfold is missing, leaving only the waiting,
And when something does occur it's always late,

Too late and incomplete, like a small residue of feeling.
We care too much about feelings—feelings for what?
Feelings can be stupid, maybe not in themselves,
But in the way they magnify and reduce, leaving you
Exhilarated and confused. I guess I'll call Diane
In a while, to see what I have to say. I could tell her
About the things I saw today: the anti-Kitty show
At the Japan Society; Shio Kusaka's white pots
With small blue dots; the drawings at the Morgan;
Eataly and the Shake Shack; these people in the window
Walking by on their way home, or God knows where.

That's the thing about time: it can take you anywhere,
And yet it takes you home. It leaves you the same person
In a different place, still always metaphysically alone,
But with friends that you can phone and tell your travels to.
I can't tell you what it is, but I can feel it flow, and flow away,
Until a memory breaks its spell and I'm in school again,
Or on a bus to college, or walking down Fifth Avenue in a
    daze.
The memory doesn't matter—what matters is the interval
It restores to life, the feeling of abstracted time made tangible,
Of duration without any destination, of a sense of a life.
I keep reading my story over and over again, my one story.
"Readers of this column are probably familiar with its details"
And I won't go over them again—they're as changeless
As the pages of those novels I keep rereading on the planes
To New York, washed in a noir California light, the scent

Of canyons after rain, the house on a canyon I won't see again.
Does it make any difference? I try to tell you these things
Not out of an urge to communicate—you have your stories
   too—
But for their own sake, and my sake too, and to make the days
   go by,
As though the point of taking stock were just to pass the time
Until there isn't any more, and the art of losing were its own
   reward.
Is that really the best one can do? To stay at home forever, living,
As Wittgenstein once put it, entirely in the present, burnishing
   the words
Until they're like a second nature, better than the first one, as
   though
Living in the moment weren't to simply let life happen, but to
   get it right?
Why is everything "as though," that great hope of the
   subjunctive life?
I ought to decide where I'm going to eat tonight. In
   Hebdomeros,
Giorgio de Chirico's novel in the form of an extended thought,
There's a passage about "those men who eat alone in
   restaurants,"
Inhabiting "the infinite tenderness, the ineffable melancholy"
Of a moment "so gentle and so poignant that one doesn't
   understand
Why all the personnel of the premises, the manager and
   cashier,

The furniture, the tablecloths, the wine jugs, down to the
    saltcellars
And the smallest objects don't dissolve in an endless flood of
    tears."
I think there's so much freedom in that thought: you stroll out
Into the night as (!) into a wilderness of traffic lights and neon
    signs.
I love feeling lost in the Village: crossing Seventh Avenue
Below West Tenth I get confused, and I love feeling confused,
Like a lamb in "The Whiffenpoof Song"—following the confusion
Wherever it may lead and (as I said a page ago) exhilarated too.
Later I can find my way back home ("wherever that may be"),
But now I'm wandering through a maze whose every prospect
    pleases,
Lingering on the curbs and corners as I make my way to
    nowhere
In particular, celebrating the end of the day with a drink and
    dinner
And a slow walk back to my hotel, pausing to look at the menu
Of a new restaurant at the end of Greenwich Avenue, across
    from
Mxyplyzyk, in the space where Café de Bruxelles used to be.

"Watchful waiting" is a way of handling prostate cancer.
It's such a gradual disease that rather than immediately rush in
With scalpels or radioactive seeds, you take a wait-and-see
    approach,
Ready for the worst if it should come to that, but meanwhile

Letting nature take its course. The worst is always on your
   mind
Of course, but at least it's not a foregone conclusion, as it is
With so many other cancers: browsing a famous blog last week
(A blog where poets seem to go to die), I saw that Paul Violi
   had died.
I'd always liked him, though I hadn't known him well. In
   January
He was diagnosed with pancreatic cancer; ten weeks later he
   was dead.
It made me think of David Sachs, a philosopher and boyhood
   friend
Of my advisor Rogers Albritton (emphysema). He'd had his
   heart set
On retiring to Scandinavia, but as retirement approached was
   diagnosed
With pancreatic cancer too, and died. It "concentrates the
   mind,"
As Samuel Johnson said of hanging, but what it concentrates
   mine on
Isn't the past I usually brood about, but the idea of the future—
Not the political future, which I've given up on, but the
   personal
Future, with its fragile possibilities and plans. Starting from the
   past
You move along a settled arc of life that leads from then to now;
But since the future isn't fixed the road that leads you on from
   there

Is open-ended, like starting out in the evening without any end
    in view.
The journey, not the distant destination; the scenes along
    the way,
And not the long look back—all great advice I guess, if great
    advice
Is what you want, instead of simply waiting for a shoe to drop.
Hello, Diane. I don't even know where I'm calling from
    anymore,
Because the scenery keeps changing: I'm wandering around
    New York,
And then I'm back in San Diego on a canyon, or I'm sitting
    on the
Deck at the Bean House, or at the Wright House in Two Rivers,
Looking at the view across the river as the fog rolls in and the
    light
Keeps changing, and the only constant is unchanging
    change.
"Unchanging change": that phrase is from "The Crystal
    Lithium,"
A poem of Jimmy Schuyler's I adore—his great long poems
    remain in
Place as they move forward, marking their time until there isn't
    any more.
I know that I'm repeating myself, yet it's precisely what I want
    to do:
There's a kind of naturalness and grace that comes with
    repetition,

With advancing by accretion through a space of rediscovered
    possibilities
Into a new world, which is the old world once removed, where
    I can
Almost imagine your face, and my face too, you to whom I write
Without writing, as though in talking to myself I also talked
    to you.
We both know life is an adventure. Death is an adventure too,
Like an experiment to be concluded in the laboratory of the
    future,
One whose outcome is completely certain, yet impossible to
    observe.
The suspense is in the details, as it morphs from an abstraction
Into something personal and real, drifting from the dark
    shadows
At the back of the mind into the bland light of an ordinary
    day.
And just as the fear of death and the unknown becomes
    diminished
By coming out into the open, so life accommodates its end
By starting over, by leaving home to find another place to live.

Where was I, and where am I now? I know of course
Exactly where I am—at the desk in my study in Milwaukee—
But that's beside the point. It's where you are in your
    imagination
That's important, for the life of simply staying where you are
Is a shadow's life, that leaves you by yourself, alone and scared.

Why can't we just move on? The light up ahead is soft
And seems to beckon us, glowing with a promise of beginning
Once again, as if there were still time. Do you remember
The "death march" along Via Veneto, and the Big Happy Bed
In Berlin? I don't think of them as memories, but as
    opportunities
To take advantage of or miss. Why don't we both revisit them,
Not to try to bring about the past, which was Gatsby's fallacy,
    but as part
Of what the future holds in store, where there might even be
    room
For that dog (although I can't imagine where)? Even Genc's,
Where all of this began, keeps pleading with us to appear once
    more
In the window over the bar and amble down the stairs. There's
    so much
Left to do, and redo, before it's time for me to show up on that
    blog—
The question is if we should make it new, or try to get it right,
Or put the question to one side and stroll once more into the
    night,
Or onto crazyJet and fly to Paris from Berlin, and check into
That terrible hotel, La Louisiane, the one you nicknamed
Hotel Claustrophobia, and make our way along the rue de
    Seine
To the Métro out to La Défense, then back to the hotel and to a
    night of
Quiet bickering over dinner at Allard. We could go there again

And stay in a better hotel, or just be less fastidious this time
    around;
Or we could visit someplace new. I've always wanted to go
To Mexico, though perhaps this isn't a propitious time. Anyway,
At least it sounds like a kind of plan, however vague. Shit,
We could go to Vegas.

                  C'mon, Diane!

BOOKS BY **JOHN KOETHE**

"Eloquent and moving . . . a fine poet."

—Charles Simic,
New York Review of Books

ISBN 978-0-06-213602-2
(paperback)

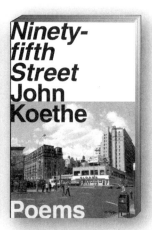

ISBN 978-0-06-176823-1
(paperback)

ISBN 978-0-06-117627-2
(paperback)

ISBN 978-0-06-093527-6
(paperback)

ISBN 978-0-06-095635-6
(paperback)

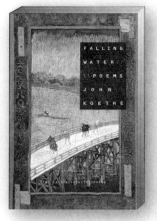

ISBN 978-0-06-095257-0
(paperback)

Visit www.AuthorTracker.com
for exclusive information on your favorite HarperCollins authors.

Available wherever books are sold, or call 1-800-331-3761 to order.